Her name is Joelle Bahdo. She is studying Cinema at the University of Zurich in Switzerland. She started writing poetry in Italian when she was 12. Writing was – and still is – a response, a coping mechanism, a defence, against all those things that were happening, and that she did not know how to express. She shifted to writing in English in 2017.

To my readers, I hope that within these pages you might find something that belongs to you as well.

Joelle Bahdo

PRIMARY POEMS

AUSTIN MACAULEY PUBLISHERS™
LONDON · CAMBRIDGE · NEW YORK · SHARJAH

Copyright © Joelle Bahdo (2020)

The right of Joelle Bahdo to be identified as author of this work has been asserted by her in accordance with section 77 and 78 of the Copyright, Designs and Patents Act 1988.

All rights reserved. No part of this publication may be reproduced, stored in a retrieval system, or transmitted in any form or by any means, electronic, mechanical, photocopying, recording, or otherwise, without the prior permission of the publishers.

Any person who commits any unauthorised act in relation to this publication may be liable to criminal prosecution and civil claims for damages.

This is a poetry book, which is a product of the author's imagination. It reflects the author's recollections of experiences over time. Any resemblance to other works of poetry, quotes, slogans, to actual persons, living or dead, or actual events is purely coincidental.

A CIP catalogue record for this title is available from the British Library.

ISBN 9781528991759 (Paperback)
ISBN 9781528991766 (ePub e-book)

www.austinmacauley.com

First Published (2020)
Austin Macauley Publishers Ltd
25 Canada Square
Canary Wharf
London
E14 5LQ

I still remember by heart the very first poem I wrote. It was spring, I was 12 and in my Italian class, my teacher told us that we had two hours to come up with a poem. We did talk about poetry for a few classes, but I was still very clueless. Here is a translation of that poem:

This year, spring is very much real/and I have two hours to write a poem/but really I have no motivation to write verses/that are already lost in my thoughts/but I can't and should not disobey/or the school director speech I would endure/so I take a piece of paper and I write down 'fruit'/my mind won't find a rhyme in this environment/I try with other words/but nothing comes to my mind/then suddenly I got an idea/I chose to talk about love/because there is no need to study/It was already time to hand in the poem/my paper was empty/the teacher already knew it/spring passed, summer arrived and the grades were given/the teacher failed me/but I wanted him to notice that/of love you cannot write but only live

I am grateful to that teacher, because if it was not for that assignment, I might have never discovered the beauty of poetry and how much it belongs to my personality.
I am also very grateful to all the people that believed in this project. Especially, to Mowgli for telling me to just do it, making it sound so simple and right that I did it.
I am as well very thankful to Austin Macauley Publishers for making this book real.

Colourless

My wardrobe is total black
my soul doesn't know how to dress

Cherishing vague hopes
silence is deafening
bathed my mind in happiness
but happiness does not imply joy

Here is a response to my feelings
I do not like to talk to them
however, they want to be heard

Stars, up there, they burn also without us
it's a little world, too dirty
too hurt
by novels, images, memories of others
people we do not belong to
too scared to be ourselves
of unreachable dreams, slaves

Just another poet
attempting nostalgia

Red

Sanguine

Noisy fragments in my bones
the tinkle of a thousand coins
no one can hear the echoes
in the holes of an empty soul

Loneliness in a glass of red
wine, blood from my hands
crumbling in writing to lovers
non-existent, to hearts

They do not beat like this
poetry of incoherent words
madly wondering around
sounds, stars and scars

The favourite cigarettes are
the ones counted as smoked
places I've never been to
are the best ones, the unknown

Attracts more than a constant
morning message, then a soft
goodnight kiss and so I'm guilty
of my broken lips, your sad eyes

Flame

Was strolling for caresses
the armour got thick instead
intoxicated by your shirt's smell
you'll never be mine
but I stayed trapped in your
big iced eyes at first sight

Bodies confused in one another
no morning was shared
your light disappeared
with the stars
a hangover coffee replaces
last night's alcohol, but not
the cigarettes, burning them
with your lighter, where are you
your hands, I sink into sheets

Sun is brightening, it's already 12
don't know how to stay, what to say
words in a poem you'll never read
distrusting love to not get hurt
we're our best adoring each other
only when the moon shines at 3 a.m.

Rose

Broken knuckles open scars
close the eyes and fix the heart
stop playing who's more though
you already won, I like you more

Of all these discrepancies
your furrowed brow, due
to a morning under pressure
the black coffee, two cappuccinos
and that drink is not the one ordered
the heavy purse empty of your dreams
at the end of every month

Projects in the pockets
bodies in love in the closet
stop hiding the thought of me
I already know, you like me more

Of all these complexes
my furrowed brow, due
to a night under pressure
the old theorem, two essays
and that grade is not the one expected
the heavy bag empty of my dreams
at the end of every month

Russet

Paralysed, I'm exhaling by
my unstable conscious
emerging from debris
that too ambitious dreams
altered my body into a vitreous one

Here, I'm lying weak and shroud
silence under water, bubbles
containing my loud thoughts
that too many times blasted by
transiting from land to land

Flouting, I'm just above embers
twinkling lights, my good memories
off by the fear of being forgotten
that too much lack of courage
transformed life into existence

Venetian Red

Trapped in the same mistakes
forever is a scar of hopes
to be deeply romantically afraid
I've never learned to handle the past

Locked up in the same room
maybe it's time to give a chance
to act like masquerades so frail
I'm still thinking about you right now

Drowned in the same silly dream
never is my answer to the stars
to get high and higher down
I've always escaped from love's future

Fire Brick

From one prison to a bigger one
facing freedom
faking certainty
fragilities and hopes

There is no good in some eyes
tempting love
trembling afraid
theatres and dreams

Escaping is the easiest way
emerging memory
emptying soul
echoes and promises

Scarlet

Inside, how many people,
names, invariably vacillating
in different shades of brown
it's not this black spiced rum

Every touch corrupts my being
violence and justice
have both carved with bloody ink
deeply in my tormented mind
trauma changes to habits

Can't you see this body
in a submarine room of ashes
empty bottles and full glasses
celebrating another instant pic?

I've been so many persons,
names, as many as I met
in different shades of yellow
I cried more days than nights

Every memory scratches my being
love and pain
have both tasted spicy in my lips
deeply to not get dressed
by regrets and by nightmares

Can't you see my eyes
invariably vacillating from pain
to pain while strolling around
empty streets, am I disappearing?

Crimson

One more drink please
to maintain the same insane
lifestyle
to keep remembering that smile
to be my own bad influence
September colours are freezing my skin
body's temperature is lowering
remember my lips only are warm

One more deal please
to hold each other's broken
knuckles
to insist in this old promise
to be my own happy version
October nostalgia is hitting my soul
breeze is whispering so sweetly
remember my love only it hurts

One more day please
to stay looking through inside
windows
to stop reflecting in those eyes
to be free from my own mind
November sky is stealing my sleep
brown leaves composing a soft bed
remember my lies only give rest

Cerise

It might have not been a loss
all of those years
all of those tears
it might have been passion
compassion more likely

Lips suspended, shouting
to the world, to your words
curled up into a soap bubble
so fragile in a dance of struggle
by a crowd furled
blazing and then, ashes
dirtied by pain
your promises, humane

The past is for the strong ones
oh, let it be, let it go
oh, forget, forgive
to repeat better the same mistake
you should have learned so much

Hands crossed, caresses
to the stars, to your scars
ripped up into nonsense poems
so strong between fresh rhymes
by a lover spelled
thrilling and then, music
shining of hope
your promises, humane

Wine

By mumbling through a glance
saying more than experienced
nestling in the loneliness of a black tea
in the waiting room of a Saturday at noon
empty in ambition like these newspapers
word has condemned imagination

By living like a fool in small talk
there's no interest in a relation
stealing love from old borderless books
in the library room of a Saturday afternoon
dust is covering like a wool blanket
wisdom has impeded youth

By hobbling in the middle of vinyl
omitting all of the bad times
drinking the usual lie the last glass
in the smoking room of a Saturday gloom
ashes between lips like soul edges
wariness has erased dreaming

Amaranth

In all of the prisons I lived
I always had the keys
victim of myself
building my reality
because what touches my body
does not give any satisfaction

I left desolation and melancholy
behind me, in that home
that used to be our castle
opening the door and pour
you wine and then your blood
I confused love, oh my beloved
for one of my obsessions, the image
of a prince that never turned to be

Waterfalls, water falls everywhere
but not a sip to quench our thirst
drops, salt our cursed souls
there are no tears no fears
wasteland, welcome to the heart
of a princess that hoped too much

Yellow

Cream

Tiny hometown full of countries
for a last night out like a movie star
white screen in front of a yellow street

Beer, coffee, of a stranger a cigarette
for a whole night out without limits
pieces of poetry and lost lovers

Sharing stars, scenes and scars
for another night out in a long take
exchanging crumbs of experience

Darkness is softening by the first light
for a night with no distance of bodies
closer attracted by that same fear

Canary

Should have caught that train
but rain has whispered to stay
something pulsed into the main vein

Curiousness twists a day's plot
a walk changes a whole mind's direction
into nature, a leaf in the city's coffee
there's yellow in the eyes and lips
chocolate frizzing with passion

Should have caught that second train
but souls are chained to the brain
mental attraction that avoiding it it's vane

Connection twists a date's plot
a vinyl changes a whole heart's rhythm
into four walls, a tea in the city centre
there's red heat between hands
love forgives who we are who we will be

Gold

Meeting halfway to see if it is real
too excited and too scared
to reach an appropriate city
on the side of the train station in a
park place surrounded by nature again

Broken jeans and a new T-shirt
a lady in yellow in a yellow car
today's style has no limit of imagination
stay in black stay in my arms like a pack
a gift to my heart that awakes it again

By trying to get you to run away
our lips ended up against each other
and it is real: the strength for uprising
not sure about how to describe this spell
it's vivid and it feels worth it to live it again

Tuscany

With a yellow T-shirt some stars away
under that same sky sitting outside
of the hotel to call me, as a friend
to talk to me as a sweet lover

So many words shared in distance
so many thoughts in one instant
so many feelings hidden in this stance

With some blue shorts some miles away
under another roof sitting inside
of that building to call you, as a lover
to talk to you as a sweet friend

So many smiles that we can only imagine
so many hugs that we can only smell in
so many feelings hidden in this stance

Honey

A sweet touch, curiousness on your lips
the same teenager's embarrassment
to feel love for the very first time
my scared heart slightly shakes

A sweet tremble, hesitant in your breath
red cheeks and cuteness all over
to feel each other's skin again
your soft heart slightly smiles

To share more nights together
under a blanket of yellow stars
a glass of wine, you and all
of the consequences is all
I want from now on till it goes

Butter

We shift from languages, miss every train
way to distracted we forgot our duties
love makes one fly up to the sky
from French to German to Italian
but it does not matter where we go
with you I feel like a shaken hurricane
hungry in the yellow bag only cookies
jumping on clouds like a butterfly
of being late you gained a medallion
but it does not matter as long you come

Here is a poem of distracted thoughts
it proves how confused I am, forget alcohol
there are too many things I want to say
to tell them you are my sun in a grey day
I do not know how to describe you to them all
you are like butter that melts in my arms only

Now, tell me if these aren't poetic shots
love makes one lose it all, slowly
like the way you kiss me in the morning
like the way I am falling in every dawning

Dandelion

In a late Sunday morning
my armour falls into crumbs
while crumbs fall into your coffee
breakfast from a yellow mug
ends in the kitchen in a big hug
and it feels like we are naked

vulnerable on the sofa
while you tell me about your past
vulnerable in the shower
while you smile about us
vulnerable in bed
while you draw on my skin
vulnerable in my arms
while you wonder where we've been

so far and now here we are
blooming like a yellow flower
a dandelion from where to wish
it feels like we have the world's power
to make a revolution from a kiss
even though here we are

fragile on the sofa
while I talk about my past
fragile in the shower
while I dream about us
fragile in bed
while I scream in a nightmare
fragile in your arms
while I say I couldn't be elsewhere

Golden Hour

Every piece of my heart directs me to you
who too fast skates from one street to the other
around these yellow fields emptied
of sunflowers, of ashes, dust, of seeds

Summer's been over since a while; however
I keep bloomin', you keep moving
stay
that I know I put too much sugar in my coffee
in my words, these iced hands that you hold
didn't meet a sweet touch since some falls ago

Violence, harder than summer's thunders
has drawn the sun's sky all over me
that kept me up for four winters thinking about
all those choices and my lack of bravery

Spring is there whenever I meet your arms
my soul waves its sourness away
stay
that you know how fragile I am in my tales
holding my breath, those sighs of strangled feelings
just found a way of flowing: through your kisses

Blue

Midnight Blue

Shivering, not out of cold
your look breathing in the cosy warmth
of your skin on mine
your smell
there are sparks from our lips
it's dark outside and the winter breeze
encloses brave souls
on the roads they walk fast
I see them from the misted window
from our crossed dreams
a kiss on the neck
a frozen hand on the back
shivering, not out of cold
your touch
breathless between sheets
white as pure is the moment
your love
and that's the last memory

Turquoise

On a thread of salt
reef cut the skin
I deceive myself in novellas
I lose roads for an avenue
blind, found myself lost
on a sea wave
run away so as not to quarrel
among the deals that of not loving
out of solitude, just to play

On a wire lulled by the sun
rays burn eyes
pages of continuous commas
outside dreams of flaky snow
defend myself against swords
on a soft lawn
an angry heart bursts
among the deals that of not hating
out of boredom, inability to stay

Sapphire

The heart has pulsed love
hitting hard on the street
without dreams a faded smile
living by waiting for the sunset
the night torment and despair
nostalgic of romance
passion in flowers that won't bloom
sky, wine, a burning wound

Sleeping without you for the first night

Words won't shut down

Between two and dawn
solitary
empty, fill
that damned silence
messy, intense, they upset me
whispered
diabolical, cut
our love
missed, distant
they remind me
of you

Bleu de France

I gave it all, I gave too much
crushing against waves
these tears
all these bodies looking at me
from my wall
representing fire and solitude
representing myself as a plenitude

You're too slow and there's no time
I was rowing
and I row, I row
my arms are tired and there're scars on my back
hoping to arise
falling, but not drowning
there's too much water
your tears

Leaving to France, to the sea
I know, you should, I see
but please stay
I row

I hate you, I adore you
I don't, but I love you
I swear
that smile
a kiss on the nose

you'll move on, it'll be about time

Indigo

Monday rain and tears
grey clouds and dirty pages
Tuesday misted windows
soaked clothes and missed words
Wednesday an uncertain smile
livid knuckles, ink all over my hands
Thursday a poem of love for sad people
afternoon at the platform, trains in delay
Friday a warm wind caresses wet faces
lit evening between wine and dances
Saturday a ray of sunshine enters the room
old photos, thinking about you since last night
Sunday I have your number but I can't call
to remind myself that it's over will hurt

Bice Blue

Fear, notes, it is night in an emotion
a range of inspiration
vibrates from the detail
ocean waves on the horizon
opaque obstacle
it's just water and salt
chills on your back
stand upright for a perspective that doesn't appear

Relief, clouds, music in a thunder
breathing in smell of rain
drawing in the snow
let yourself go
lightly
the bitterness brought by the breeze,
painless dreamt kiss
tighten up before it is distant
the past, a safe place, a lover that doesn't disappear

Periwinkle

We share memories
so many, we belong
between screams and deaf hearts
pride makes fun of us
joking about old notes of passion
what happened to that revolution, eh?

We play hide and seek
I'm cold inside
a lonely body has no warmth
the skin burns with pain
do you know how many nights, how many hours
wishing you were here
while you sleep, dreams away?
I'm here writing a story
that will remain ink
crazy-poetry

I hate having every reason to despise you
but always find an excuse to love you

Majorelle Blue

Like a rift on the wall
crumbling by anger and pain
frustration of a life without a destination
the madness of indecision
between white flag and revolution

A stain of red wine on my favourited white shirt
certain passions are not removable
an indelible pencil, an illusion
in the doubt of a giant mistake
I'm an admiral without a ship
I have the keys but no treasure chest
and you know I cannot breathe
time is taking it all, oxygen and hope

Should I wait or should I break it?

Cerulean

Nervousness devours me from the bones
I feel you
but I don't remember your perfume
smoking the past
hit the walls, broken knuckles
I know, I know I had stopped
to love you, to smoke, to hurt me

I swear I didn't want to
but it burns in the arteries
flames, flames, flames
damn
I miss you

I run, I run, I run
I run away and look away
but everyone already knows
it was love at first sight
and now there is rain from the eyes
I wait for you in vain and without patience

We might meet again in another place
one with walls empty of memories

Zaffre

It is not over, not yet, I know
you'll be better they say, they say wrong
here there are only ashes to swallow
no more dandelions to blow

There were red leaves on the trees
turned yellow on the street, there is
a cold sun up in the sky and breeze

Yesterday night you called
told me about your new favourite store
all the stairs to the Tour Eiffel
told me you missed me even more

My heart beats and beats
at every beat breaks
cracks a bit

Come here, reach me by train I changed
come to Paris, I'll show you Monet, no chains
we will walk around, it's fall, quit the pain
for one day we will be us, free and the same

Primary Colours

You took me to an empty museum
at a new platform
it is an art project
you say while taking pictures
with an old camera to white walls
our first night sitting at the white screen

Can we start it all over again, please?

I know, my eyes are sad, your lips are broken
we danced last night until the wine was over
the unknown, promises of no return, left to France
but to sleep on your shoulder is mine romance

Let's paint these walls, let's get dirty again, at ease?

I have them all
red, yellow and blue

You met me that I was an empty soul
with pastels you draw me in, the whole
love that you had: a fire, a sunflower and the sea
you draw until I fell in love, until I believed

I have all the colours, let me draw in you
we can start from today, it's white
let it be a rainbow, let it be us again